Afternoons and Afterwards

FOR PIANO   John McCabe

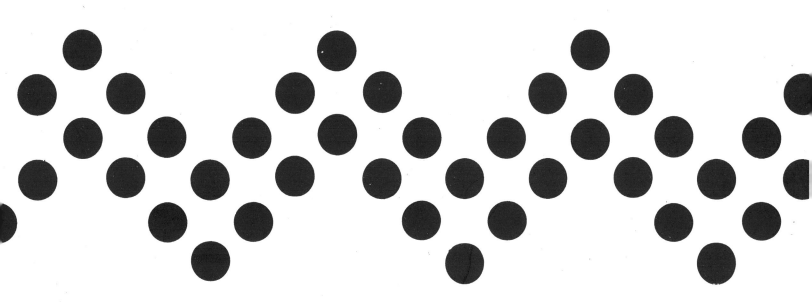

Order No. Nov 100246

NOVELLO PUBLISHING LIMITED
14-15 Berners Street, London W1T 3LJ

CONTENTS

page

1 Swans at Stratford 2
2 On the beach 4
3 Champagne Waltz 6
4 Sports car 9
5 A game of darts 12
6 Forlane 14
7 The Artful Dodger 16

Total duration 10¾ minutes

Introduction

The gap between starting to learn an instrument and playing 'real' music is a very great deterrent to many players. Consequently, I, and some other composers got together to tackle this problem.

We are producing a series of pieces for many different instruments, playable by musicians with limited technical ability. As a guide, each has a grading similar to those of the Associated Board of the Royal Schools of Music, but I hope people of all grades will enjoy playing them.

Richard Rodney Bennett

Richard Rodney Bennett
Series Editor

To Patti
AFTERNOONS AND AFTERWARDS
for piano
by
JOHN McCABE

1 SWANS AT STRATFORD

Lento, grazioso ♩ = *c.* 80

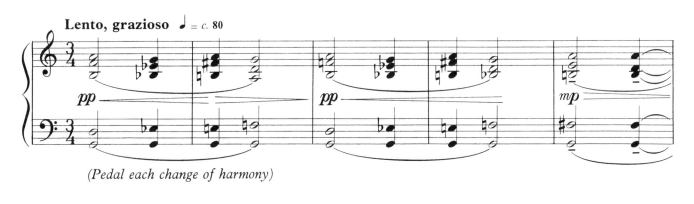

(Pedal each change of harmony)

2 ON THE BEACH

Moderato, piacevole ♩ = c. 58

1' 40"

6

3 CHAMPAGNE WALTZ

L.H.

rall.

Ped.

1′ 35″

4 SPORTS CAR

con Ped.

1' 40"

5 A GAME OF DARTS

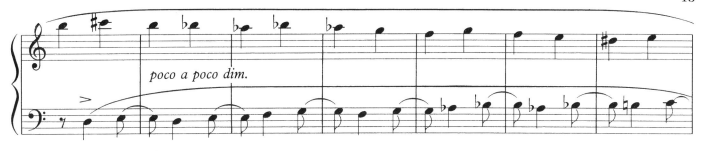

55"

6 FORLANE

7 THE ARTFUL DODGER

Allegro ♩ = c. 132